Seeking Pure Relationships

Making Right Choices

To the Graduate

*Y*our life stretches out before you like a long runway—a runway capable not only of propelling you into the vast sky above but of revealing new and exciting places and opportunities beyond your wildest dreams.

Between you and the distant horizon is a whole new world. Some of it you'll merely glide over—enjoying the breathtaking view from afar; occasionally you'll take the time to land and explore. This new world and all these opportunities summon you to get going, to take off on your own journey.

But no matter how far you can see ahead, or how well you've charted your course, you can't determine exactly how you will get to where you want to go. There's always that unexpected storm, or that extremely high mountain range, that keeps you from knowing which route you should take.

Life doesn't offer any guarantees. You don't know what to expect, but you do know there will be times when you will have to make difficult decisions. There will be times when you'll have to decide whether you should make that rough landing or keep flying in spite of the bad weather.

Taking Flight

Wisdom for Your Journey

Elisabeth Elliot

Baker Books

A Division of Baker Book House Co
Grand Rapids, Michigan 49516

© 1999 by Elisabeth Elliot

Published by Baker Books
a division of Baker Book House Company
P.O. Box 6287, Grand Rapids, MI 49516-6287

Fourth printing, February 2003

Printed in the United States of America

Library of Congress Cataloging-in-Publication Data

Elliot, Elisabeth
    Taking flight : wisdom for your journey / Elisabeth Elliot.
      p. cm.
    ISBN 0-8010-1180-9 (cloth)
    ISBN 0-8010-6357-4 (paper)
      1. College graduates—Religious life. 2. Young adults—Religious life.
    3. College graduates—Conduct of life. 4. Young adults—Conduct of life.
    5. Christian life. I. Title.
    BV4529.2.E55 1999
    248.8′34—dc21   98-48301

The selections in this book are taken from the following books
by Elisabeth Elliot:
All That Was Ever Ours (ATW)   Passion and Purity (PP)
Discipline: The Glad Surrender (D)   Quest for Love (QL)
God's Guidance (GG)   The Mark of a Man (MM)
On Asking God Why (AGW)

Unless otherwise indicated, Scripture references are from The New English
Bible. Copyright 1961, 1970, 1989 by The Delegates of Oxford University Press
and The Syndics of the Cambridge University Press. Reprinted by permission.
Other versions quoted include the King James Version (KJV), the New Interna-
tional Version® NIV® (NIV), the Revised Standard Version (RSV), and the New
Testament in Modern English, Revised Edition (Phillips).

For current information about all releases from Baker Book House, visit our
web site:
                      http://www.bakerbooks.com

For Tomorrow, Too

The books are closed.
The sun streams into the library,
And I stand,
Pensive,
Looking beyond the Tower
To the green horizon.
The years have been full—
How transient, they!
Yes, "you'll never forget
Your college days . . . "
"You step into a cold world . . . "
Perhaps.
But there is no difference—
The days, Lord, have been Thine.
Thy "Lo, I am with you" is
For tomorrow, too.
Let us remember the way.
But make us press on.
Give us true gratitude
For all the blessing;
Give us pure vision.
Show us the path of life.

ELISABETH HOWARD, AGE 21
JUNE 1948

Contents

*abbreviation for book title—see copyright page for explanation

There will even be times when you'll feel like you're flying in circles, unsure of where God is leading you.

Elisabeth Elliot is an experienced guide for the adventure you face. She has dedicated her life to God and has triumphed in spite of unexpected twists and turns (most notably the tragic death of her newlywed husband in 1956 at the hands of Auca Indians).

In this slender volume you'll find a treasure trove of Elisabeth Elliot's wisdom for your life's journey. You'll learn how to deal with doubt, worry, and loneliness. You'll learn how to recognize and wait for God's best for you. You'll learn how to align your hopes and dreams with God's plan for your life. You'll discover that total surrender to God is not the easiest course, but it's the only course that brings true joy and fulfillment.

The author doesn't offer instant advice or pat answers, because she knows that the mysteries of life defy simple, quick-fix formulas. Instead she invites you to come alongside her and watch how she has dealt with the joys and heartaches of life.

Following
the
Guide

Old Testament writers made much of the name of God. Israel was a nation specifically set apart as a place for God to put His name. Appeals were made on the basis of the name. "For thy name's sake lead me, and guide me," the psalmist prayed. Not because of who I am, not in recognition of my reputation, but because of who You are. "And his name will be called 'Wonderful Counselor.'" "The Lord is my banner." "Lord God of Hosts." No questions of merit can arise with regard to that name. It is above every name. Therefore I can come today on the ground of that name's merit.

The prayer that Jesus taught His disciples begins with the petition, "Our Father who art in heaven, hallowed be thy name." Whatever our requests may be that bring us to His feet, they should begin with a careful consideration of the meaning of this form of address. If we say the words slowly and thoughtfully, they cannot help but color the rest of the prayer. If it is guidance we are asking, we may be very wrong in our hopes as to the direction it will take. We may be ill-prepared in heart for the road God will choose for us. But, as George MacDonald wrote: "The thought of Him to whom that prayer goes will purify and correct the desire."

If we did not have God's unequivocal promise, the words, "Guide *me*, for the sake of *Your* name" would sound outrageously presumptuous. But the truth is that God said He would do just this. There is nothing presumptuous or precarious about it. The validity of the divine word is at stake, and that is a very sure foundation.

*T*here are those who do not want to receive Christ. Those who do, however, are given not an "instant kingdom" but the "right to *become* children of God." Here is the truth of divine sovereignty and human responsibility wrapped up in a single verse. To those who *will* He gives. There are many levels of meaning here that we cannot explore. It does not say God makes them instant children of God. It says He gives them the right to become. To those who receive Him, to those who have yielded to Him their allegiance, He gives the right to *become* children of God.

If we hold back our obedience until we have plumbed the theological depths of this mystery, we shall be disobedient. There are truths that cannot be known except by doing them. The Gospels show many cases of those who wished to understand rather than to obey. Jesus had scathing words for them. On one occasion He turned from them to those who had already believed in Him and said, "If you dwell within the revelation I have brought, you are indeed my disciples; you shall know the truth, and the truth will set *you* free" (John 8:31–32).

The Bible does not explain everything necessary for our intellectual satisfaction, but it explains everything necessary for our obedience and hence for God's satisfaction.

To those who will He gives.

Meeting God

The Bible is God's message to everybody. We deceive ourselves if we claim to want to hear His voice but neglect the primary channel through which it comes. We must read His Word. We must obey it. We must live it, which means rereading it throughout our lives.

We read that our Heavenly Father actually looks for people who will worship Him in spirit and in reality. Imagine! God is *looking for* worshippers. Will He always have to go to a church to find them, or might there be one here and there in an ordinary house, kneeling alone by a chair, simply adoring Him?

When I stumble out of bed in the morning, put on a robe, and go into my study, words do not spring spontaneously to my lips—other than words like, "Lord, here I am again to talk to You. It's cold. I'm not feeling terribly spiritual." Who can go on and on like that morning after morning, and who can bear to listen to it day after day?

I need help in order to worship God. Nothing helps me more than the Psalms. Here we find human cries—of praise, adoration, anguish, complaint, petition. There is an immediacy, an authenticity, about those cries. They speak for me to God—that is, they say what I often want to say, but for which I cannot find words.

Surely the Holy Spirit preserved those Psalms in order that we might have paradigms of prayer and of our individual dealings with God. It is immensely comforting to find that even David, the great king, wailed about his loneliness, his enemies, his pains, his sorrows, and his fears. But then he turned from them to God in paeans of praise.

He found expression for praise far beyond my poor powers, so I use his and am lifted out of myself, up into heights of adoration, even though I'm still the same ordinary woman alone in the same little room.

We have ample evidence that the Lord is able to guide. The promises cover every imaginable situation. All we need to do is take the hand He stretches out. But it is here that the hardest question arises for me. How, exactly, do I take His hand? Isn't this an extreme oversimplification of the conditions of the promises?

I know He has said over and over, "I will guide you." I know the words, "It is the LORD who goes before you; he will be with you, he will not fail you or forsake you; do not fear or be dismayed" (Deut. 31:8 RSV). But there are so many promises with conditions attached, conditions that seem impossible to fulfill for us who are not far along the road to sainthood. Often I have prayed to God for light, and He has shown me some promise in the Bible that indicates He will certainly give me the light I am asking for, *if*—and then I have found, to my despair, that a great deal is asked of me in exchange. Who does

God think I am, that I can meet such demands before He will answer my prayer?

The first condition is the recognition of God Himself. It is not who does He think I am, but who do I think He is. I confess that after many years I am still having to go back often to this, to Lesson One in the school of faith. I forget what I learned. I started out on false premises: who I am, what I need, why my case is special, what I'm hoping for, what I pray for, or something—anything but the thing that matters most: who God is.

I have called this—the recognition of who God is—the first condition. Perhaps it would be better to call it the primary condition, for it is not one we can fulfill once and for all and then move beyond. The recognition of who God is is a lifetime process. Nor does it end with our earthly life. "This is eternal life, that they know thee the only true God, and Jesus Christ whom thou hast sent" (John 17:3 RSV).

When I am looking for the right direction, I ought to take into account what experience I have had, what gifts or propensities are mine, and what the direction of my life heretofore seems to have prepared me for.

It is a scriptural principle that the divine energy acts upon the stuff of this world. Jesus had the servants fill the stone jars that happened to be standing there when He made wine from water at the marriage in Cana. He used a boy's lunch, instead of starting from nothing, to feed five thousand people. His own spittle and the dirt at His feet were the remedies for a blind man's eyes. Common things taken into the divine hands accomplished eternal purposes.

The nature of the thing in question is obviously important. Jesus . . . does not by any means disregard the sort of person we are when He calls us to do His will. He knows our frame and remembers that we are dust. He knows the weaknesses and strengths, the tastes and fears and prejudices and ignorance and experience of each of us. What He wants to make of us, if we are willing to be made over, is sure to bear a relationship to what we are when we first come to Him. It is within His power to transform. It is for us to submit to the transformation.

I have said earlier that God often isolates a man in order to reveal Himself. It is when alone that a man most clearly recognizes God for who He is. But it is in relationship with his fellowmen that he comes to know himself. Seeking the will of God as though it had nothing to do with anybody else leads to all kinds of distortions.

What is in my hand? What is my function in the Body of Christ? Have I something to give? Can I see a place where it is needed now? These questions will help me to know what I ought to do.

*H*ow in the world can I find out what God wants me to do, if I don't know what *I* want to do?" you may ask. Why not start by simply telling God you'll do anything He says? You're the servant. He's the master. It's the only reasonable approach, isn't it? Furthermore, there *is* the possibility that what He says will be something you'd like.

There are over a million pregnancies per year among unmarried girls under twenty. What they want they take, any way they can get it. Where do they learn this? Some of them, sadly, from their parents, who have shed the responsibility of marriage, home, and children for another "life-style," another partner, another career, another bid for the happiness that will always elude them. If a mother or father, by behavior, says in effect, "It's my life, this is what I want, forget the rest of you," their children will follow suit. Who shows them another way?

There is another way: to love what God commands and desire what He promises. It can't be found except through prayer and obedience. It cuts across quite the other way, takes us where things are not at the mercy of changing fashions and opinions. It is a place where a man's heart may safely rest—and a woman's heart, too.

*Love what God commands
and desire
what He promises.*

We need never ask the question, "How do I know I'm called?" We ought rather to ask, "How do I know I am *not* called?" We are required to take the risk, move, trust God, make a beginning. This is what Jesus always asked of those who came to Him for help of any kind. Sometimes He asked them to state their case ("What do you want Me to do?"), to affirm their desire ("Do you want to be healed?"), and often to *do* something positive ("Stretch out your hand") before He could do His work. There had to be evidence of faith, some kind of beginning on their part. The first baby step of faith is followed by a daily walk of obedience, and it is as we continue with Him in His Word that we are assured that we were, in fact, called and have nothing to fear.

The most common fear of the true disciple, I suppose, is his own unworthiness. When Paul wrote to the Corinthians, a group of Christians who had made some terrible messes even inside the church itself, he still never doubted their calling; for they were prepared to hear the Word and to be guided and corrected. It was not the *perfection* of their faith that convinced him they were called. They had made a beginning. In that beginning, Paul found evidence of faith: "It is in full reliance upon God, through Christ, that we make such claims. There is no question of our being qualified in ourselves: we cannot claim anything as our own. The qualification we have comes from God" (2 Cor. 3:4–5).

Desire and conviction both play a part in vocation. Often the desire comes first. There may be a natural inclination or an interest aroused by information or perhaps an unexplained longing. If these sometimes-deceptive feelings are offered to the Master and subjected to the test of His Word, they will be confirmed by various means and become a conviction. Sometimes the conviction comes first, accompanied not always by desire but by fear or dread, as in the case of the Old Testament prophets who were given very hard assignments. The only thing to do then is arise and go.

*I have called thee
by thy name;
Thou art mine.*

hen Mary went to the garden tomb on the first Easter morning, she did not know the Lord right away. She took Him to be the gardener until He spoke her name. That brought recognition. Instantly she responded, "Master!" (And we know by those two forms of address, "Mary" and "Master," something important about their relationship.)

In Isaiah we read, "Thus saith the LORD that created thee, . . . I have called thee by thy name; thou art mine" (43:1 KJV).

How shall we hear that call? Some in our own day have heard voices, we are told, but I am not one of them. There has never come to me anything audible. But I have found that the Lord knows how to call us. (Strange that I should be surprised at that!) He knows the best way to get our attention, and if we are ready to listen or to be shown, we will hear or see whatever it is He has chosen as His means.

God's Timing

*I*t is reasonable to expect that God will use whatever means may be appropriate *at the time*. The time I refer to is God's time, not ours. We will know when we need to know, not before.

When I review "all the way which the Lord my God hath led me"—those segments of the way I can remember because they seemed to me significant—I realize that nearly all of my trouble with finding out the will of God came because I wanted it too soon. I like to plan. I like to have things mapped out well in advance, and uncertainty of any sort puts me on edge. Perhaps it is for this very reason God has often asked me to wait until the last minute, right up to what looked like the screaming edge, before I found out what He wanted me to do.

My acceptance of His timing was a rigorous exercise in trust. I was tempted to charge the Lord with negligence and inattention, like the disciples in the boat in a storm. They toiled frantically until the situation became impossible, and then instead of asking for Jesus' help they yelled, "Master, don't you care that we're drowning?" They weren't perishing, they were panicking. It was not too late. Jesus got up and merely spoke to the wind and sea.

On that other occasion, many centuries earlier, when the power of God to command water was what was needed to lead His people, the priests of Israel actually had to get their feet wet before God did anything. Why does He put us to this kind of test? Probably to give us the chance to make a conscious act of faith, often a specific, physical act, a move of some kind toward Him. "And when . . . the feet of the priests bearing the ark were dipped in the brink of the water . . . the waters coming down from above stood and rose up in a heap."

Sometimes we are in a quandary because we have already been shown what we ought to do and we are not satisfied with it. We are saying, "Lord, when are You going to tell me?" and the truth is that He has told us.

Sometimes the word comes very slowly. In Psalm 112:4 we read, "Light rises in the darkness for the upright" (RSV). It may be a gradual thing, imperceptible at first as the coming of the dawn, but long before we see it, the cock crows and there are stirrings. There is no question at all that the dawn will come. We have only to wait.

Questioning God

*T*here are those who insist that it is a very bad thing to question God. To them, "why?" is a rude question. That depends, I believe, on whether it is an honest search, in faith, for His meaning, or whether it is a challenge of unbelief and rebellion. The psalmist often questioned God and so did Job. God did not answer the questions, but He answered the man—with the mystery of Himself.

He has not left us entirely in the dark. We know a great deal more about His purposes than poor old Job did, yet Job trusted Him. He is not only the Almighty—Job's favorite name for Him. He is also our Father, and what a father does is not by any

God is my Father still, and He does have a purpose for me.

means always understood by the child. If he loves the child, however, the child trusts him. It is the child's ultimate good that the father has in mind. Terribly elementary. Yet I have to be reminded of this when, for example, my friend suffers, when a book I think I can't possibly do without is lost, when a manuscript is worthless.

In all three I am reminded that God is my Father still, that He does have a purpose for me, and that nothing is useless in the fulfillment of that purpose—if I'll trust Him for it and submit to the lessons.

What Is Faith?

*D*r. James I. Packer, in his book *God's Words*, says "The *popular* idea of faith is of a certain obstinate optimism: the hope, tenaciously held in face of trouble, that the universe is fundamentally friendly and things may get better."

I would have had to be an optimist of the most incorrigible obstinacy to have held on to that sort of faith in the dark times of my own life. It has been another faith that has sustained me—faith in the God of the Bible, a God, as someone once put it, not small enough to be understood but big enough to be worshipped.

If we believe that God is God, our faith is not a deduction from the facts around us. It is not an instinct. It is not inferred from the happy way things work. Faith is a gift from God, and we must respond to Him with a decision: The God of the universe has spoken, we believe what He says, and we will obey.

We must make a decision that we will hold in the face of all opposition and apparent contradiction.

The powers of hell can never prevail against the soul that takes its stand on God and on His Word. This kind of faith overcomes the world. The world of today must be shown. We (you and I) must show them what Jesus showed the world on that dark day so long ago—that we love the Father and will do what He says.

The Redemption of Creation

One day I was surprised to find a lone gull sitting on our deck. There was something odd about the way he sat, and the shape of his head. Moving to the window I saw that he had the plastic rings from a six-pack of drinks clamped in his bill and circling his neck. He sat very quietly, a little hunched, his head tipped inquiringly. He was caught in the rings, unable to close his beak. Was he perhaps, by daring to perch on our deck, asking for help? Slowly I opened the door and tiptoed toward him. His fierce bright eyes followed me unblinking, but he did not move. When, incredulous, I nearly touched him, off he flew.

That ninety seconds or so on our deck brought to focus once more a phrase I turn over and over in my mind: the redemption of creation.

"Redemption? But animals have no *souls*!" someone objects. Have they not? My Bible tells me of a great hope shared not only by angels and men and women but "all things, whether on earth or in heaven" (Col. 1:20); it tells me that *all* is to be "brought into a unity in Christ" (Eph. 1:10). What can this mean if not that in some way unimaginable to us now the suffering seagull, along with all feathered, furred, scaled, and carapaced creatures, will be redeemed? "The universe itself is to be freed from the shackles of mortality" (Rom. 8:19). Will not our ears someday hear the Song of the Animals? I think so. I pin my hopes on the vision of John: "Then I heard every created thing in heaven and on earth . . . and in the sea . . . crying, 'Praise and honor and glory and might, to Him who sits on the throne and to the Lamb for ever and ever!'" (Rev. 5:13).

The Mystery of Evil

*E*vil men have often been permitted to do what they please. We must understand that divine permission is given for evil to work. To know the God of the Bible is to see that He who could have made automatons of all of us made instead free creatures with power and permission to defy Him.

There is a limit, of course. Let us not forget this. The Tower of Babel was stopped. God has set limits on what man is allowed to do, but one day He put Himself into men's hands. Jesus had sat in the temple teaching and nobody touched Him, but the time came when the same people who had listened to Him barged into Gethsemane with swords and cudgels. Jesus did not flee. He walked straight up to them. He was unconcerned about physical safety. His only safety was the will of the Father. "This is your moment," He said, "the hour when darkness reigns" (Luke 22:53).

Why did God make room for that moment? Why should there ever be an hour when darkness is free to rule?

When Jesus refused to answer Pilate the next morning, Pilate said, "Surely you know that I have authority to release you, and I have authority to crucify you." Jesus' reply embraces the mystery of evil: "You would have no authority at all over me if it had not been granted you from above" (John 19:10–11).

Every man and woman who chooses to trust and obey God will find his faith attacked and his life invaded by the power of evil. There is no more escape for us than there was for the Son of Man. The way Jesus walked is the way we must walk.

Flesh Becomes Word

*W*ords are inadequate, we say. So they often are. But they are nonetheless precious. "A word fitly spoken is like apples of gold in pictures of silver." In a time of crisis we learn how intensely we need both flesh and word. We cannot do well without either one. The bodily presence of people we love is greatly comforting, and their silent companionship blesses us. "I know I can't say anything that will help, but I wanted to come," someone says, and the word they would like to speak is spoken by their coming. Those who can't come send, instead of their presence, word. A letter comes, often beginning, "I don't know what to say," but it is an expression, however inadequate, of the person himself and what he feels toward us.

Before Eve heard the voice of the serpent summoning her to the worst possibility of her being, before Adam heard the voice of God summoning him to his best, the Word was. The Word was at the beginning of things, the Word was with God, the

Word was God. That Word became visible in the
flesh when the man Christ came to earth. Man saw
Him, talked with Him, learned from Him, and when
His flesh was glorified and He returned once more
to His Father, men declared what they had seen.
"That which was from the
beginning, which we have
heard, which we have seen
with our eyes, which we
have looked upon and
touched with our hands,
concerning the word of life
. . . we proclaim also to you"
(1 John 1:1, 3 RSV). That
eternal Word had become
flesh, and through those who knew Christ that flesh
had become once more Word. Those who hear that
Word today and believe it begin to live it, and again
it becomes flesh.

Forget the past.
Press toward
the goal.

*I*n this world," Jesus said, "you will have trouble. But take heart! I have overcome the world" (John 16:33 NIV). None of us likes pain. All of us wish at times that we need not "go through all this stuff." Let's settle it once and for all: We cannot know Christ and the power of His resurrection without the fellowship of His suffering.

Often with that thought arises another: Can *my* sufferings have anything to do with His? Because my fickle feelings bring turmoil and sorrow in my life, can I nevertheless hope for some small share in that divine fellowship? The apostle Paul helps us here. He had known many kinds of severe suffering that were directly related to his work for God (and few of our afflictions, I suppose, would fall into *that* category), yet even he says, "Forgetting what is behind and straining toward what is ahead, I press on toward the goal to win the prize for which God has called me heavenward in Christ Jesus" (Phil. 3:13–14 NIV).

By the grace of God, we can will to do His will. Forget the past. Press toward the goal.

Taking Up Your Cross

*A*ll our problems are theological ones, William Temple said. All of them have to do with our relationship to God and His to us, and this is precisely why it makes sense to come to God with them.

The taking up of the cross will mean sooner or later saying no to self. But it is also a resounding yes. It means saying yes when everything in us says no. To decide to do the thing that we (and, it will seem, everybody else in the world) do not want to do because it is not "natural." And in our giving of wholehearted assent, we find to our amazement that the impossible becomes possible and the things we were sure were beyond us are now within reach, for God's command is His enabling. *Never* has He given an assignment that was not accompanied by the power to accomplish it.

The cross entails sacrifice, too. There is no getting around this. Christianity has been criticized and rejected by many as an "unnatural" religion, a life that denies living, a negation and not an affirmation. Jesus never tried to make it look easy. The principles He taught cut across the grain of human nature: lose your life in order to find it; be poor in spirit if you want to be happy; mourn if you want to rejoice; take the last place if you want the first. The corn of wheat must first fall into the ground and die if it is ever to produce anything.

What we must not forget is that He traveled this road before us. "He himself endured a cross and thought nothing of its shame"—not because He had a particular liking for self-denial and suffering but "because of the joy he knew would follow his suffering. . . . Think constantly of him enduring all that sinful men could say against him, and you will not lose your purpose or your courage" (Heb. 12:2–3 *Phillips*).

The Glad Surrender

As a child in a Christian home, I did not start out with an understanding of the word *discipline*. I simply knew that I belonged to people who loved me and cared for me. That is dependence. They spoke to me, and I answered. That is responsibility. They gave me things to do, and I did them. That is obedience. It adds up to discipline. In other words, the totality of the believer's response is discipline.

While there are instances where the words *discipline* and *obedience* seem to be interchangeable, I am using the first as comprehending the second and always presupposing both dependence and responsibility. We might say that *discipline* is the disciple's "career." It defines the very shape of the disciple's life. *Obedience*, on the other hand, refers to specific action.

Discipline is the believer's answer to God's call. It is the recognition, not of the solution to his problems or the supply of his needs, but of *mastery*. God addresses us. We are responsible—that is, we must make a response. We may choose to say yes and thus fulfill the Creator's glorious purpose for us, or we may say no and violate it. This is what is meant by moral responsibility. God calls us to freedom, fulfillment, and joy—

but we can refuse them. In a deep mystery, hidden in God's purposes for man before the foundation of the world, lies the truth of man's free will and God's sovereignty. This much we know: A God who is sovereign chose to create a man capable of willing his own freedom and therefore capable of answering the call.

Jesus, in response to the will of the Father, demonstrated what it means to be fully human when He took upon Himself the form of a man and in so doing voluntarily and gladly chose both dependence and obedience. Humanity for us, as for Christ, means both dependence and obedience.

The unwillingness on the part of men and women to acknowledge their helpless dependence is a violation of our "creatureliness." The unwillingness to be obedient is a violation of our humanity. Both are declarations of independence and, whether physical or moral, are essentially atheistic. In both, the answer to the call is no.

Discipline is the wholehearted yes to the call of God. When I know myself called, summoned, addressed, taken possession of, known, acted upon, I have heard the Master. I put myself gladly, fully, and forever at His disposal, and to whatever He says my answer is yes.

A New Creation

I've already blown it. The standard is impossible. No way can I start picking up the pieces now," some of you may say.

Do our transgressions disqualify us for the Christian life? Quite the contrary. Jesus came into the world specifically for us who blew it, not for those who "need no repentance." "He was wounded for our transgressions."

If sexuality is a paradigm of the Heavenly Bridegroom and His pure and spotless Bride, how shall we who are impure and badly spotted start over again? "Make no mistake: no fornicator or idolater, none who are guilty either of adultery or of homosexual perversion, no thieves or grabbers or drunkards or slanderers or swindlers, will possess the kingdom of God," Paul wrote to the Corinthian Christians (1 Cor. 6:9–10). Sounds as though there isn't much chance for any of us. But then he says, "Such were some of you, but you have been through the purifying waters; you have been dedicated to God and justified through the name of the Lord Jesus and the Spirit of our God" (v. 11). He goes on in his next letter to say, "For the love of Christ leaves us no choice, when once we have reached the conclusion that one man died for all and therefore all mankind has died. His purpose in dying for all was that men, while still in life, should cease to live for themselves, and should live for him who for their sake died and was raised to life" (2 Cor. 5:14–15).

This teaches us that there is a point of departure. What we were and what we are in Christ are sharply distinct. Stop living for yourself; start living for Christ. Now.

"With us therefore worldly standards have ceased to count in our estimate of any man; even if once they counted in our understanding of Christ, they do so now no longer. When anyone is united to Christ, there is a new world; the old order has gone, and a new order has already begun" (2 Cor. 5:16–17).

*T*he tabernacle, in ancient times, was a myste-
rious representation of certain eternal concepts
that Israel was not yet equipped to understand. The
priests were the stewards of those mysteries. Like-
wise, the husband, as priest in his home, is charged
with the guarding of mysteries. It's his business to
remember what marriage represents—the heavenly
union of Christ and His Bride—and to pay attention
to the everyday means of living this out with the
woman God gave him.

Often the attempt will seem so laughable, such a
travesty, so ludicrously unlike what it stands for,
that both will wonder how God could possibly have
laid such a solemn task at their door. If the toast is

burning, the phone ringing, the baby pouring milk down the mother's back, and the husband frantically trying to find his briefcase in time to make the car pool, he will not, at the moment, feel much like a "trustee of the mysteries." But he is one nevertheless. "No one takes this honor upon himself; he must be called by God," the writer to the Hebrews says (5:4 NIV).

You wouldn't choose it for yourself, but if you remember that you're called by God to the work, and if you witness to that calling in the home you establish, it will be a saving, even a life-transfiguring, reality.

You're called by God to the work.

Seeking Pure Relationships

Matters of the Heart

*H*earts do break. The same hearts are breakable over and over again.

Is there anywhere to turn but to Him who "heals the brokenhearted and binds up their wounds" (Ps. 147:3 NIV)? Broken hearts are not new to Him, and His power is limitless, for He is the One who numbers the stars and calls them all by name (vs. 4). Have you noticed these two verses that juxtapose God's concern for the wounded *and* His numbering and naming the stars? His compassion and His power are mentioned together that we might understand that the Lord of the Universe is not so preoccupied with the galaxies that He cannot stoop to minister to our sufferings.

He has a glorious purpose in permitting the heartbreak. We find many clues for this in Scripture. For example:

- that we may be shaped to the likeness of Christ (Rom. 8:29)
- that we may learn to trust (2 Cor. 1:8-9)
- that we may learn to obey (Ps. 119:67, 71)
- that we may bear fruit (John 15:2)

- that we may reach spiritual maturity
  (James 1:4)

Our sufferings are not for nothing. Never. However small they may be, we may see them as God's mercy in giving us the chance to unite them with His own sufferings. Christ suffered for our sins and we suffer because of the sins of others (and they suffer because of ours). There is a mystery here, far deeper than our understanding, but we may take it on faith, on the authority of the Word, and believe it will not go for nothing.

A broken heart is an acceptable offering to God. He will never despise it. We do not know what unimagined good He can bring about through our simple offering. Christ was willing to be broken bread for the life of the world. He was poured out like wine. This means He accepted being ground like wheat and crushed like the grape. It was the hands of others who did the grinding and crushing. Our small hurts, so infinitely smaller than His, may yet be trustfully surrendered to His transforming work. The trial of faith is a thing worth much more than gold.

God created Adam first. Then, seeing the one thing that He labeled "not good" in His creation—that the man should be alone—He created a creature marvelously like and marvelously *unlike* that man.

She was made *for* the man.
She was made literally *from* the man ("bone of his bone").
She was brought *to* the man.
She was named *by* the man.

Was she not "equal" to the man? Yes—in three specific ways:

Both were made by God.
Both were made in the image of God.
Both were placed under moral responsibility.

But the two are also notably "unequal" and, as I see it, *gloriously* unequal. Not competitive but complementary, Have you watched a man and a woman waltzing? We did, in Vienna—a professional pair. What beauty! What grace! What harmony and complementariness! What a lovely paradigm of graceful rule and glad submission! If the woman had suddenly made up her mind to lead, the whole thing would have been hideously botched.

Adam was given the privilege of naming the woman God gave him. This implied, as it did with his naming the animals, his acceptance of authority. Godly authority is intended to build up rather than to pull down (see 2 Corinthians 10:8). Adam was also assigned the responsibility to care for, pro-tect, provide for, cherish, and *husband* his wife.

She was made to be his helper, comforter, lover.

He was to initiate, she was to respond.

But the roles were quickly reversed. Eve took the initiative in disobeying God by eating the fruit of the Tree of the Knowledge of Good and Evil, a fruit forbidden by the Lord because He had not created the man and the woman to sustain the terrible burden of such knowledge. Eve took the word of the serpent as more trustworthy than God's, and Adam went along with it.

She initiated. He responded. Sin, sorrow, and death were the result.

Is Chastity Possible?

*T*o choose chastity has always been possible, because "The one who is in you is greater than the one who is in the world" (1 John 4:4 NIV).

The "traditional" view has been handed down to us by no less an authority than God Himself, yet it is deeply disturbing to find that abstinence, chastity, virginity, sexual purity are seldom the subjects of sermons in most churches today. It is often taken for granted that, as free moral agents, we may choose whatever feels good or seems "right" for us.

But God's word is plain. "God did not call us to be impure, but to live a holy life" (1 Thess. 4:7 NIV).

A holy life is a whole life.

56

A holy life is a *whole* life. The words *whole* and *holy* derive from the same root.

The very struggle in which we find ourselves when sexual longings are unfulfilled is *God's call*: Come to ME. I will give you rest. But we must take *His* yoke—a burden indeed, but a light one, He promises. It is much lighter than the yoke our self-will imposes. Until Jesus Christ is Lord of the sex life He is not Lord of one's *life*. Not only is every act meant to be subject to His holy will, but every thought must be brought into captivity to Christ. And this "captivity" turns out to be JOY!

A scientist named Freeman Dyson described some early experiences in the laboratory. He was delighted to be turned loose with crystals and magnets and prisms and spectroscopes to work through some famous old experiments, knowing beforehand how things were supposed to behave. It was in the Millikan oil-drop experiment that he had a revelation.

Robert Millikan, a physicist at the University of Chicago, was the one who first measured the electric charge of individual electrons. He made a mist of tiny drops of oil and watched them float around under his microscope while he pulled and pushed them with strong electric fields. Dyson, following Millikan's rules, had gotten the drops floating nicely when he grabbed the wrong knob to adjust the electric field. They found him stretched out on the floor.

This brief and nearly fatal exposure to an immutable law revealed to him what Einstein had meant when he said, "The eternal mystery of the world is its comprehensibility." Dyson realized that his most elaborate and sophisticated calculations about how an electron *ought* to behave would do nothing more than show how it *would* behave, regardless of whether or not he ever bothered calculating its actions. The electrons in the oil drop knew exactly what they were supposed to do and did it—to his peril, when he took hold of the wrong knob.

We're living in a dangerous time. People are tampering with God's arrangements, grabbing the wrong knobs. The results are not always so dramatic and so instantaneous as they were for Dyson, but they are equally inexorable: Sow the wind; reap the whirlwind.

I have been in close touch with several married couples who are in deep difficulty because, I believe, they have been infected with the theory that masculinity and femininity are not very important. They have "tampered with the wrong knobs," so to speak, by denying God-given gifts, trying to make husband and wife "equal" and/or interchangeable. Rhetoric about liberation and mutual submission and egalitarianism sounds harmless enough, even enlightened; but it is perilous in the extreme, and people are ending up "on the floor," as it were. There *is*, in fact, an arrangement for men and women, just as surely as there is one for electrons.

Einstein saw the world as comprehensible—that is, he recognized its design and predictability, which were, in themselves, its very mystery. Shall we who acknowledge the world's Creator deny that most tremendous of human mysteries: the design for sexuality? Shall we focus instead on something attenuated and poor, something legally or (worse!) sociologically defined?

*S*ometimes you hear people say that sex is "a perfectly natural function," meaning that it is no different or no more important than eating and drinking. They're dead wrong. People throughout history have known what a whole lot more is at stake here than in other "natural functions." That's why sex has always been surrounded with ceremony and sanctions and rules and taboos and secrecy.

Anybody who contemplates sexuality for as much as five minutes knows that he is up against a mystery. Who can understand all that is implied in that renunciation, that new establishment, that intimacy? Who can explain the dynamics between a man and a woman? Solomon, the wisest man who ever lived, confessed himself beaten:

> Three things are too wonderful for me;
>   four I do not understand:
> the way of an eagle in the sky,
>   the way of a serpent on a rock,
> the way of a ship on the high seas,
>   and the way of a man with a maiden.
>   Proverbs 30:18–19 RSV

The apostle Paul, too, admitted that there was much more in marriage than he could fathom.

Some feminists treat marriage as though it were a diabolical plot. "We must reform and abolish the institution of legal marriage," Gloria Steinem said. The Declaration of Feminism, drawn up in Minneapolis in 1972, stated, "Marriage has existed for the benefit of men. The end of the institution of marriage is a necessary condition for the liberation of women. We must work to destroy it."

Clearly such women are adrift. Yet other women follow them, blindly hoping that what they are offering is freedom and fulfillment. The awful truth is that what they offer is bondage and destruction; for they would strip us all—men and women alike—of all mystery and, indeed, of our very humanity. You can't be human and not be a sexual creature. You can't be human and not be made in the image of God. You can't be human and not be a bearer of mystery. You can't be man in relation to a woman and not be skirting very close to one of the deepest mysteries of all.

The Discipline of Waiting

*I*s there a harder discipline than that of waiting, especially when one's desires seem as wild and uncontrollable as a prairie fire?

Without real trust in who God is—trust in His never-failing love and wisdom, we set ourselves up for disappointment. Is He a good God? Will He give what is best? If the answer is yes to both questions, it follows that He will withhold many things that look attractive to us. It is His mercy to withhold them. Shall we accuse Him of failure to get "His act" together or shall we echo the psalmist's word, "I am still confident of this: I will see the goodness of the LORD in the land of the living. Wait for the LORD; be strong and take heart and wait for the LORD" (Ps. 27:13–14 NIV).

If we imagine that happiness is to be found by furious pursuit, we will end up in a rage at the unsatisfying results. If, on the other hand, we set ourselves to pursue the wise and loving and holy will of our Heavenly Father, we will find that happiness comes—quietly, in unexpected ways, and surprisingly often, as the by-product of *sacrifice*.

Waiting is a form of suffering—the difficulty of self-restraint, the anguish of unfulfilled longing, the bewilderment of unanswered prayer, flesh and heart failing, soul breaking. These are indeed tribulations, and tribulation is the curriculum if we are to learn patience. We want answers *now*, right *now*, but we are required at times to walk in darkness.

Nevertheless, God is in the darkness.

"My soul, wait thou only upon God; for my expectation is from him" (Ps. 62:5 KJV). In Him alone lie our security, our confidence, our trust. A spirit of restlessness and resistance can never wait, but one who believes he is loved with an everlasting love and knows that underneath are the everlasting arms will find strength and peace.

God is in the waiting.

Lord, you have assigned me
my portion and my cup;
you have made my lot secure.

Psalm 16:5 NIV

The Gift of Singleness

*I*f you are single today, the portion assigned to you *today* is singleness. It is God's gift. Singleness ought not to be viewed as a problem, nor marriage as a right. God in His wisdom and love grants either as a gift. An unmarried person has the gift of singleness. Unless you are bound by the gift of celibacy (a vow not to marry), what may be your portion tomorrow is not your business today. Today's business is trust in the living God who precisely measures out, day by day, each one's portion.

Those who long for the gift of marriage can find great peace in the words of Psalm 16:5, receiving *one day at a time* the divinely apportioned gift of singleness, believing that our Heavenly Father's love will withhold nothing that is *good* for us.

It should not be forgotten that a lifetime of singleness may be His choice for us. Will we still love Him, trust Him, and praise Him?

What to Do with Loneliness

*B*e still and know that He is God. When you are lonely, too much stillness is exactly the thing that seems to be laying waste your soul. Use that stillness to quiet your heart before God. Get to know Him. If He is God, He is still in charge.

Remember that you are not alone. Jesus promised His disciples, "Lo, I am with you always" (Matt. 28:20). Never mind if you cannot feel His presence. He is there, never for one moment forgetting you.

Give thanks. In times of my greatest loneliness I have been lifted up by the promise of 2 Corinthians 4:17, 18, "For this slight momentary affliction is preparing for us an eternal weight of glory beyond all comparison, because we look not to the things that are seen but to the things that are unseen." This is something to thank God for. This loneliness itself, which seems a weight, will be far outweighed by glory.

Refuse self-pity. Refuse it absolutely. It is a deadly thing with power to destroy you. Turn your thoughts to Christ who has already carried your griefs and sorrows.

Accept your loneliness. It is one stage, and only one stage, on a journey that brings you to God. It will not always last.

Offer up your loneliness to God, as the little boy offered to Jesus his five loaves and two fishes. God can transform it for the good of others.

Do something for somebody else. No matter who or where you are, there is something you can do, somebody who needs you. Pray that you may be an instrument of God's peace, that where there is loneliness you may bring joy.

The important thing is to receive this moment's experience with both hands. Don't waste it. "Wherever you are, be all there," Jim once wrote. "Live to the hilt every situation you believe to be the will of God."

Making Right Choices

To search out and sort out all the whys and wherefores of what we call our problems (a few of which just might be plain sins) may be one route to the healing of certain kinds of human difficulties, but I suggest that it may be the longest way home. I say this, I know, at the risk of being labeled simplistic, reductionist, obscurantist. But where, I want to know, does genuine understanding begin?

> But where can wisdom be found?
> And where is the source of understanding?
> No man knows the way to it:
> It is not found in the land of living men.
> The depths of the ocean say, "It is not in us,"
> and the sea says, "It is not with me."
> Red gold cannot buy it,
> nor can its price be weighed out in silver.
> . . . God understands the way to it,
> he alone knows its source. . . .
> And he said to man:
>> The fear of the Lord is wisdom,
>> and to turn from evil is understanding.
> Job 28:12–15, 23, 28

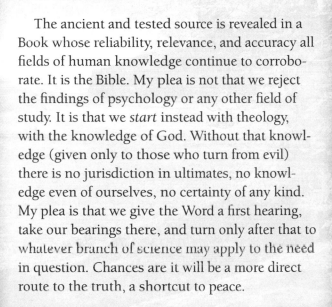

The ancient and tested source is revealed in a Book whose reliability, relevance, and accuracy all fields of human knowledge continue to corroborate. It is the Bible. My plea is not that we reject the findings of psychology or any other field of study. It is that we *start* instead with theology, with the knowledge of God. Without that knowledge (given only to those who turn from evil) there is no jurisdiction in ultimates, no knowledge even of ourselves, no certainty of any kind. My plea is that we give the Word a first hearing, take our bearings there, and turn only after that to whatever branch of science may apply to the need in question. Chances are it will be a more direct route to the truth, a shortcut to peace.

*O*ne particular spot where I lived as a missionary became like a "place of dragons." It was full of things I was afraid of and did not know how to cope with. Once in a while I felt as though I were about be devoured. "Sore broken" is the psalmist's expression, and I thought I knew how he felt. I was on my way back to that place one night, camping where we usually did at the junction of two rivers. The Indians had made me a reed hut to sleep in and had finished their own hut-building, fishing, eating, and talking. Everything was quiet except for the night birds and tree frogs. There was nothing especially distinct about this journey back home. I had made it before. But as I lay in my blanket I began to feel something like what fell on Abraham: "a horror of great darkness." How could I go back to those "dragons"? My heart was about to turn back.

Then I thought of Jesus' words to His disciples: "Lo, I am with you all the days." If He was with me then I was certainly with Him. The place of dragons was the place He was taking me, and I was still following—I had not gotten off the track. I was with Him still, sharing in a small measure His cross.

Never for a second does God lose sight of His objective. It is we who forget what it is. We are distracted by immediate circumstances, and it is no wonder we want to give up the whole thing. It was the "joy that was set before Him" that enabled Jesus to endure the cross.

Without a clear understanding of the ultimate objective, the intermediate objectives make no sense to us. "Why this, Lord?" we keep asking. But if we bear in mind that we shall, beyond any doubt whatsoever, finally dwell in the house of the Lord, settle down to stay in His presence, then the intermediate pastures and waters, even the valley of the shadow or the place of dragons, are understood. They are stations and landings along the journey, and they will not last long.

Overcoming Worry

*F*rustration is not the will of God. Of that we can be quite certain. There is time to do anything and everything that God wants us to do. Obedience fits smoothly into His given framework. One thing that most certainly will not fit into it is worry. Here are six reasons why:

1. Worry is totally fruitless. Have you ever succeeded in adding an inch where you wanted it, or subtracting one where you didn't want it, merely by being anxious? If you can't accomplish that by worrying, what *can* you accomplish?
2. Worry is worse than fruitless: it is disobedience. Note these commands: Fret not; fear not; let not your hearts be troubled; be not dismayed; be of good cheer.
3. Worry is taking the not-given—for example, tomorrow. We are allowed to plan for tomorrow, but we are not allowed to worry about it. Today's troubles are enough of a burden. Jesus knew exactly what He was talking about when He said that.

4. Worry is refusing the given. Today's care, not tomorrow's, is the responsibility given to us, apportioned in the wisdom of God. Often we neglect the thing assigned for the moment because we are preoccupied with something that is not our business just now. How easy it is to give only half our attention to someone who needs us—friend, husband, or little child—because the other half is focused on a future worry.

5. Worry is the antithesis of trust. You simply cannot do both. They are mutually exclusive.

6. Worry is a wicked squandering of time (as well as energy).

Direct your time and energy into worry, and you will be deficient in things like singing with grace in your heart, praying with thanksgiving, listening to a child's account of his school day, inviting a lonely person to supper, sitting down to talk unhurriedly with wife or husband, writing a note to someone who needs it.

*B*e still, and know that I am God."

If we have once kept silent long enough to know this, we have, at least in that moment, been ready to obey. But it is the being still that is so hard for us. It often takes illness, loss, suffering of some kind, isolation, and loneliness. Only when we have come to the end of our own resources, when few distractions are left to us, does it become possible to be quiet.

But if, in the providence of God, we have not yet had to weather a real crisis, we may "be still" on purpose. We may choose to obey the command, stop all activity, turn aside in stillness, and know. The best kind of beginning, when we are wanting to know the will of God, is to concentrate first on God Himself. And of course, the briefest effort to do this will humble us, for we will learn how poorly we are in control of our thoughts. For me, there is nothing like the printed word to help me corral my scattered thoughts. Simply looking at a verse in the Bible that tells me something of God and reading through a hymn or a prayer are aids to discipline, and I need all the aids I can get.

I have been told that in one of the China Inland Mission homes in China there was a motto on the wall that said, "The sun stood still. The iron did swim. This God is our God for ever and ever. He will be our guide even unto death." This God, the One who, in answer to the prayer of an ordinary man, stopped the sun in its course, the God who suspended His own law of gravity and made an ax head float, this is the God to whom I come. This is the God whose will and direction I am asking. This God is the One whose promises I am counting on. Whatever my predicament may be, as soon as I compare it with the circumstances surrounding the miracles of the sun and the ax, my doubts seem comical.

God knows all about those comical doubts. He knows our frame. He remembers that we are dust, and it is to us, knowing all this better than we know it ourselves, that He made those promises.

God is, according to Isaiah 43, our Creator, our Redeemer, the Lord our God, the Holy One of Israel, our Savior. Would we ask Him to be anything more than this, before we admit in our hearts that He can be trusted?

Self-Deception

*T*he old English word denoting that part of us which constantly wars against the spirit is *flesh*. Yet the story of Jesus' life reveals that He was a man, really a man, fully a man. We know He was sinless, so we must conclude that there was absolutely nothing inherently sinful in the physical stuff of which His body was made—the bone, muscle, tissue, blood. There is nothing sinful in our bone, muscle, tissue, or blood either.

What is it then that is at war with the spiritual life? Can we be human and holy at the same time? The question came to the fore in my lucubrations about Jim. My love for him was human. I wanted it also to be—I hoped and prayed that it would be—holy.

There is room for self-deception here. It is possible to deny the strongest human drive, sexuality, and to spiritualize what is a thoroughly natural and human hunger for marriage.

Paul did not deceive himself about the power of women over men or vice versa. He knew the drives, was acquainted with the pitfalls, and very sensibly told the Christians of Corinth, "It is a good thing for a man to have nothing to do with women; but because there is so much immorality, let each man have his own wife and each woman her own husband" (1 Cor. 7:1). In other words, when you get to the point where you can't keep your hands off each other, it's time to get married.

Let's be candid with ourselves before God. Call a spade a spade or even a muddy shovel. If your passions are aroused, say so—to yourself and to God, *not* to the object of your passion. Then turn the reins over to God. Bring your will to Him. Will to obey Him, ask for His help. He will not do the obeying for you, but He will help you. Don't ask me how. He knows how. You'll see.

The Tyranny of Change

*T*here are many things we want to be liberated from, many kinds of tyranny from which we would like to escape, but one of the inescapable ones is the tyranny of change. (I didn't make up that idea. I got it from Paul, reading the Phillips' translation of Romans 8:20–21.)

Most of us are ambivalent about change. We say, "Let's do this for a change," and in the next breath moan, "Oh dear, how things have changed! They're just not the same anymore." Lots of people do things purely for the sake of doing something different. And one of the ironies is that things don't necessarily turn out to be all that fresh and original after all.

I don't like change very much. I am not always moving the furniture around. I don't want any "bright new taste surprises" for breakfast. I want the sofa where it was yesterday and the black coffee just the way I always make it.

It was reassuring to me to learn that C. S. Lewis also liked monotony and routine. Urged time and again to journey abroad to lecture,

he stayed home and smoked his pipe and lectured where he felt he belonged. He also wrote wonderful things and remained content with familiar surroundings, able to draw on deep inner resources.

We need not be always seeking something different, something other, out of mere restlessness. There are enough changes we cannot stop, which are of the essence of this life and are meant to be. They are meant to drive us to God.

The world of creation, said Paul, has, in God's purpose, been given hope. "And the hope is that in the end the whole of created life will be rescued from the tyranny of change and decay, and have its share in that magnificent liberty which can only belong to the children of God."

*A*n ancient longing for danger, for challenge, and for sacrifice stirs in us. We have been insulated from having to watch others suffer by putting them where somebody else will do the watching and from guilt by calling any old immorality a "new morality." We don't risk involvement if we can help it. We try not to turn around if somebody screams. Responsibility for others we'd rather delegate to institutions, including the government, which are supposed to make it their business to handle it.

I saw a man on television telling us that what America needs is a little more honesty. Because of technology, the man said, people have to be more dependent on each other than they used to be (Oh?) and therefore we need more honesty (Oh). Probably, he allowed, our standards have never been quite what they ought to be and it's time to hike them up a notch or two.

How do we go about this? Take a deep breath and—all together now—start being honest? Ah, the man had a plan. I waited, tense and eager, to hear what it might be. Popularization was what he proposed. Make honesty the In Thing. If everybody's doing it, it will be easy. In fact, it would take the *risk* out of it.

Funny, I always thought righteousness was supposed to be risky. I was taught it wasn't easy, and I found it hard when I tried it. It's never likely to be either easy or popular.

I'm for civilization. I'm all for certain kinds of progress and I accept quite gladly most of today's means of avoiding the risks, but to imagine that we shall whip off the dishonesty that is characteristic of fallen human nature everywhere as painlessly as we whip off one garment and put on another, to imagine that by simply taking a different view we shall come up with a no-risk brand of honesty, is a piece of self-deception and fatuity to make the mind reel.

Plato, three hundred years before Christ, predicted that if ever the truly good man were to appear, the man who would tell the truth, he would have his eyes gouged out and in the end be crucified.

That risk was once taken, in its fullest measure. The man appeared. He told the world the truth about itself and even made the preposterous claim "I am the Truth." As Plato foresaw, that man was crucified.

He calls us still to follow Him, and the conditions are the same: "Let a man deny himself and take up his cross."

The Risks of Witnessing

*W*itnessing means obedience. Every time you do what God says to do or refuse to do what He says not to do you witness to the truth. And witnessing to the truth is a very risky business—risky in the world's terms. You're likely to be arrested, Jesus predicted, handed over to prison, brought before governors, and kings. Aleksandr Solzhenitsyn, Dietrich Bonhoeffer, Corrie ten Boom, and thousands of others know what He meant. They also understand what He said next: "Hold on, and you will win your souls. In the world you'll have tribulation, but cheer up, I have overcome the world."

Witnessing conquers the world, but it doesn't exempt you from suffering. Witness enables others to see what they could not otherwise have seen. It changes the picture. Think of Stephen. He never minced any words. Standing before the highest civil and religious court of the Jewish nation, called the Sanhedrin, he witnessed. He spoke the plain truth about Israel's history.

If miracles didn't persuade them, what would Stephen's defiance do? They ground their teeth at him in a rage and stoned him to death. But while the rocks were flying, Stephen saw something. He saw heaven opened, he saw the glory of God, and Jesus Himself standing at His right hand. That's witness. It conquers the world. It makes truth visible. It changes the picture.

When we see Stephen we see not the fury of the religious Jews, not the rain of stones falling on his head, but a man beholding the Lord. Faith stands in the midst of suffering and sees glory. The Church is here not to deliver us from suffering—and I believe you young men and women will be called to suffer. The Church will make witnesses, those who see the promises of God, the angel in the lion's den, the Son of Man in the flames, Jesus standing up to welcome His beloved Stephen.

Heroes

*O*f the many young people who tell me that Jim
    Elliot's life has inspired their lives, it is sur-
prising how many carefully preface their remarks
with disclaimers such as, "I don't mean he's a hero
or anything."

Well, what is a hero, anyway? "Any man admired
for his courage, nobility, or exploits, the central fig-
ure in any important event, honored for outstanding
qualities." Wasn't Jim a hero? We badly need heroes.
How else shall we grasp the meaning of courage or
strength or holiness? We need to see such truth
made visible in the lives of human beings, and Jim
did that, it seems to me.

Heroes are paradigms. They show us what
strength or courage or purity actually *looks* like.

Jesus was a hero in that sense. Consider His last night before the Crucifixion. After praying the great prayer of John 17 He had gone with the disciples to the garden. Judas arrived with the guard and officers. They came with lanterns and torches and weapons. A man's natural instinct would be to flee.

"Jesus, fully realising all that was going to happen to him, went forward and said to them, 'Who are you looking for?'" (John 18:4 *Phillips*). It was a demonstration of quiet courage, born of the knowledge that He was held by the sovereign will of His Father.

How else shall we grasp the meaning of courage or strength or holiness?

Choosing the Harder Path

_M_ost of us avoid crises when we can. It is far
more comfortable to sit in the back row than
to stand up and be counted. To take up the cross
and follow, to walk in the light, to climb "the steep
ascent of heaven" are not options that have a strong
popular appeal.

But we are speaking of those who actually want
to do the will of God. What we are concerned with
now is the business of choice when both alterna-
tives seem equally moral.

Choose the harder of the two ways. If you have
eliminated all other possibilities and there still seem
to be two that might please God, choose the more
difficult one. "The way is hard, that leads to life,"

Jesus said, so it is likely that He is asking us to will against our will.

But what if He isn't asking that? The more sincerely we seek the will of God, the more fearful we will be that we may miss it. If it made little difference to us, obviously we would not worry very much about it, so there ought to be a measure of reassurance for us in the very fact of our fear. Jesus is in the boat with us, no matter how wild the storm is, and He is at peace. He commands us not to be afraid.

The supreme example, outside that of our Lord Himself, of a man willing against his own will, in obedience to God, is Abraham. He was asked to sacrifice Isaac, his only son—and this, in the face of all God's promises about descendants. Abraham was to tie the boy down on top of a pile of kindling on an altar. This he did (with what anguish we can only imagine), and only then, when with the knife poised he had triumphantly passed the hardest test of faith, did God show him that his son's death was not finally required.

I have finished
the work
You gave me

*T*he Christian attitude toward work is truly revolutionary. Think what it would do to the economy and the entire fabric of life if the question were asked daily: "Who is your Master?" and the answer were given: "Christ is my Master, whose slave I am." It would transform in a stroke not only the worker's attitude toward the boss, but his attitude toward those who work with him. He would not be seeking ways to evade work that he doesn't like. It would change his attitude toward the work itself because he would do it with single-mindedness, for Christ. It would change the quality of the work, for he has a master who sees every detail of the work done and the intentions of the heart.

Think of the brightness there will be in the place where work is done for God. Think of the peace in the heart of the workman who lifts it up to Him. We will finish our course with joy if we stick to the assignment. We will be able to say as Jesus did, "I have finished the work you gave me."

Honoring God with Our Wealth

*F*ew of us are as well acquainted with the extremes that the apostle Paul knew: "I know what it is to be brought low, and I know what it is to have plenty. I have been very thoroughly initiated into the human lot with all its ups and downs, fullness and hunger, plenty and want." In whatever measure we have experienced these, the Lord has given us opportunity to learn the vital disciplines of possessions.

The first lesson is that things are *given by God*. "He did not spare his own Son, but gave him up for us all; and with this gift how can he fail to lavish upon us all he has to give?" (Rom. 8:32).

The second lesson is that things are given us *to be received with thanksgiving*. Faith looks up with open hands. "You are giving me this, Lord? Thank you. It is good and acceptable and perfect."

The third lesson is that things can be *material for sacrifice*. This is what is called the eucharistic life. The Father pours out His blessings on us; we receive them with open hands, give thanks, and lift them up as an offering back to Him, thus completing the circle.

This lesson leads naturally to the fourth, which is that things are given to us *to enjoy for a while*.

Nothing has done more damage to the Christian view of life than the hideous notion that those who are truly spiritual have lost all interest in this world and its beauties. The Bible says, "God . . . endows us richly with all things to enjoy." It also says, "Do not set your hearts on the godless world or anything in it." It is altogether fitting and proper that we should enjoy things made for us to enjoy. What is not at all fitting or proper is that we should set our hearts on them. Temporal things must be treated as temporal things—received, given thanks for, offered back, but *enjoyed*. They must not be treated like eternal things.

And there is a fifth lesson: *All that belongs to Christ is ours.* As Amy Carmichael wrote, "All that was ever ours is ours forever."

We often say that what is ours belongs to Christ. Do we remember the opposite: that what is His is ours? That seems to me a wonderful truth, almost an incredible truth. If it is so, how can we really "lose" anything? How can we even speak of His having the "right" to *our* possessions?

"Son, thou art ever with me, and all that I have is thine," the Father says to us. That is riches.

Hope, a Fixed Anchor

*C*hristian hope is a different sort of thing from other kinds. The real essence of the word is *trust*.

When Lazarus died, the hopes of his two loving sisters, Mary and Martha, were dashed. Jesus, hearing the news, did not hurry to the house but stayed where He was for two more days. When He finally got to Bethany both sisters greeted Him with the same words: "If only You had been here, Lord!"

Jesus said, "I Myself am the resurrection." This is our hope. It is a living thing. It is, in fact, Christ Himself. It is also something to live by. When our hopes for healing or success or the solution to a problem or freedom from financial distress seem to come to nothing, we feel just as Mary and Martha did. Jesus might have done something about it, but He didn't. We lie awake thinking about all the "if onlys." We wonder if it is somehow our fault that the thing didn't work. We doubt whether prayer is of any use after all. Is God up there? Is He listening? Does He care?

Mary and Martha had envisioned His coming and raising a sick man from his bed. He came too late. Unfortunately Lazarus was dead—so dead, Martha pointed out, that decomposition would have set in. It had not crossed their minds that they were about to see an even more astonishing thing than the one they had hoped for—a swaddled corpse answering the Master's call and walking, bound and muffled, out of the tomb.

The truth of the story is that God knew what was happening. Nothing was separating the grieving women from His love. He heard their prayers, counted their tears, held His peace. *But He was faithful, and He was at work.* He had a grand miracle in mind.

The duration of my suffering may be longer than that of Lazarus's sisters, but if I believe, trust, flee to God for refuge, I am safe even in my sorrow, I am held by the confidence of God's utter trustworthiness. He is at work, producing miracles I haven't imagined. I must wait for them.

*F*lannery O'Connor wrote a story about a Civil War veteran 104 years old whose granddaughter Sally Poker Sash is about to graduate from college at the age of sixty-two. The general didn't give two slaps for her graduation with its long procession of teachers and students. He liked parades with floats of Miss Americas and Miss Daytona Beaches and Miss Queen Cotton Products but he didn't have any use for processions, and a procession full of schoolteachers was about as deadly as the River Styx to his way of thinking.

There is probably a lot of sympathy in the audience today for General Sash's way of thinking. We have largely lost the idea of ceremony, and the word *pomp* has come to be used mostly in a bad sense—"all that pomp and circumstance stuff" we hear people say, usually with a sneer. But there is deep significance in our reserving special garb and special music and a special pace for occasions like this. I doubt if anyone comes dressed in academic regalia today simply because he feels it is remarkably becoming. Cap and gown is not, I'd venture to say, "your thing." But you didn't get where you are merely by doing your own thing. You've been doing somebody else's thing, and you wear these robes today precisely because they are somebody else's thing—symbols of old traditions which represent the discipline and the dignity of learning. These robes represent not vanity and self-conceit but obedience. Today we agree to the dignity not because it fits us necessarily—we are in fact keenly conscious of how unfitted we really are—but we are obedient to something beyond and much bigger than ourselves.

I've entitled my talk today "My Name on That List." What list? We have in our hands a very important list indeed, and every one of you scanned it the minute you got it to make sure your name was on it, and spelled right. If your name was not there you knew it was a mistake, because it belonged there. Your parents or somebody paid the many thousands of dollars, which is a pretty impressive sum to educate one man or one woman, and some of you may have a sneaking suspicion that you might not be worth all that, but somebody paid the money, and you yourself did the work, with a lot of help from a lot of sources. You got on this list at last, and you got there by obedience to authority, by submission to a certain set of rules, partly social and partly academic, but rules which define what this college is all about, so that when you go out of here you go out as a graduate of this institution and your name will stay on their lists as long as they can keep track of you.

You want always to be proud of them, and they want to be proud of you. They are proud of you today. That's why we're here—the beaming aunts and grandparents, the proud younger brothers and sisters, the ecstatic parents, the well-wishing friends, and the relieved professors. We're here not to put you down but to celebrate. The pomp and the ceremony are not for nothing. They're a special way of remembering. They embody, in a formal way, some important facts which this college and your parents and everybody else who has paid a price of any kind to train you do not want you to forget.

But there is another list I have in mind. It has a bizarre assortment of people on it—a devout shepherd, a five-hundred-year-old father of three, a wealthy Chaldean, a Hebrew reared in an Egyptian palace, and a harlot. They are not on the list because they took the right number of credit hours. One of them is there because of a sacrifice he made, another because of a massive carpentry project, another an illogical journey, another an impossible mission, and the harlot because she took a dangerous risk. The names were Abel, Noah, Abraham, Moses, and Rahab. The list is found in the eleventh chapter of Hebrews, and these people got on it for one reason: faith. The things they're remembered for, things God inspired men to preserve in the record for all time, were things done by faith, actions based on principles which are invisible. In other words—obedience.

Listen to some verses from Hebrews 11 (*Phillips*): "It was because of his faith that Abel made a better sacrifice to God than Cain. It was through his faith that Noah constructed an ark. It was by faith that Abraham obeyed the summons to go out and [here some of you will feel very much like Abraham] he set out in complete ignorance of his destination. It was by faith that Abraham, when put to the test, offered Isaac for sacrifice. [By faith Moses] looked steadily at the ultimate reward. By faith he left Egypt; he defied the king's anger with the strength that came from obedience to the invisible king. And what other examples shall I give? There is not time to continue [and I'm still quoting here from Hebrews—this is not me talking] by telling the stories of Gideon, Barak, Samson, and Jeptha; of David, Samuel, and the prophets. Through their faith these men conquered kingdoms, ruled in justice and proved the truth of God's promises. They shut the mouths of lions, they quenched the furious blaze of fire, they escaped from death by the sword." That's where the quotation ends. Suppose we add to the list "By faith the class of _____ changed the climate of the century. By faith the students of this college subdued urban violence; wrought racial, economic, and social justice; established a righteous government; restored ecological balance; and made peace in the world." Some of you smile, some of you slump into the boredom you came prepared to slump into. That is the sort of speech you expect to hear from a commencement speaker—they always talk about bright young faces, sharp young minds, boundless youthful energy, the hope of the world. Every class that's ever graduated from anything has, I suppose, expected to hear something akin to that. This class, I'm sure, is accustomed to being told that you belong to the most formidably intelligent generation the world has ever seen. You've been flattered and listened to with round-eyed attention by your elders—your parents, perhaps, but certainly by many of your teachers from kindergarten upwards. "Tell us how you feel. How do you really feel about everything? What do you think of the new sandbox, of the hot lunch program, of having homework, of supervised study halls, of saluting the flag, of the curriculum, of dormitory hours or compulsory chapel or the cut system or exams or even of your professor's professional performance?" And you have had all kinds of chances to sound off in class and out, in student forums and panels and the student newspaper and now you're on your way out of here, some perhaps with the cheery assumption that the world waits to hear from you, others with the uneasy apprehension that nobody's going to be listening anymore.

Is it likely that this class will change the climate of the age? There may be one or two whose names will go into the history books. There will be more than that, I trust, who by the faithful performance of their work of whatever kind will change their own immediate world. But the older you get the more disenchanted you will be with the potentialities of committees and organizations and politics, necessary as these things are. How much, in the long run, can be done by groups and institutional machinery? The wheels grind exceedingly slowly, and the most selfless dedication on the part of some will be offset by the lust for power on the part of others, and the machine will seem to move with the speed of a glacier. But then on the other hand, what can one man accomplish alone? The possibilities here seem even more bleak.

Ladies and gentlemen, make no mistake about it. The kind of work that changes the world, the really transforming work, is done not by a new use of power or by intellectual brilliance or by the mobilization of ever larger and more concerned forces but in the last analysis by sacrifice. The formula for the most enduring kind of success is the formula Jesus Himself gave us: "I tell you truly that unless a grain of wheat falls into the earth and dies, it remains a single grain of wheat; but if it dies, it brings a good harvest. The man who loves his own life will lose it, and the man who hates his life in this world will preserve it for eternal life. If a man wants to enter my service, he must follow my way" (John 12:24–26 *Phillips*).

The people who got on the list in Hebrews were not waited for by the world. Nobody would have known where to look for them. Nothing could have been expected from such a collection. They were people who in vastly different ways exercised faith in the same Almighty God and put their own lives on the line for the sake of that faith. They were irresistible in their obedience, steadfast in their suffering, resolute in the face of risks even when the risks entailed their lives, their families, their families' lives, their reputations, and in two cases it seemed the reputation of God Himself—how could Abraham lash that beloved son to an altar and raise the deadly knife when God's promise that he would be the father of many nations was at stake? How could Moses consent to an impossible mission when the name of the great I AM would be derided by a heathen potentate?

But some of you know that Hebrews passage well enough to know that I didn't read the whole list. I stopped just where most of the Sunday School books would stop. We all love the stories that ring with triumph: shutting lions' mouths, quenching furious fires, and escaping from death. But there's a lot more to this business of faith. There's another whole category we're not allowed to leave out. Let me read that part: "And others were tortured to death. Others were exposed to the test of public mockery and flogging, and to being left bound in prison. They were killed by stoning, by being sawn in two" (vv. 35–36 *Phillips*).

Christianity is no lyricism. The faith that bore those heroes down into the depths of darkness and suffering was not—and I hope you will remember this if you remember nothing else—*that faith* was not their own thing. They didn't drum it up. They didn't somehow work themselves up to it by getting to know themselves or love themselves or by doing what they felt like doing. It came from a Source outside themselves, outside the sphere of this world's understanding, from the One who said, "Without Me you can do nothing." Nothing, that is, that would ever get you on that ageless list.

Many decades have passed since a young man named Jim Elliot graduated from college with highest honors in Greek. He hadn't been known on the campus only for his studiousness. He was good-looking, he was likable, he could be a clown and recite Robert Service's poems, "The Shooting of Dan McGrew" or "The Face on the Barroom Floor," he got a prize for beard-growing back when nobody would be caught dead with a beard, and he was a champion wrestler in four states. He did something else that nobody on campus knew about. He kept a diary which he gave me permission to read when I became his wife. This is what he wrote in his junior year: "Father, take my life, my blood if Thou wilt. Have it, Lord, have it all. Pour out my life as an oblation for the world." He couldn't possibly have known how that prayer would be answered. He couldn't have imagined then that eight years later he and four friends would be speared to death on a jungle riverbank. The first-person account of what happened on that bloody beach in 1956, taped for me by two Auca Indians who actually plunged in the spears, takes you back to the last half of that Hebrews list. "And others." Tortured, stoned, sawn in two. This faith of which we talk so much—is it a feeling? Feelings wouldn't have been enough for Abraham or for those five.

May I ask you to look steadily at what faith meant for the people on the list I've been talking about? May I ask you to be as realistic as you have ever been in your life?

Maybe you've been told you're the world's most brilliant generation. Think about the generations that produced da Vinci, Abelard, Galileo, or Pascal. Some of you may think you've been born into a world with bigger problems. Think about the kids who grew up during the Black Plague. Forget the bill of goods sold to you by the mass media. Look soberly at yourselves before God. Not many of you will find it easy to picture yourselves shutting lions' mouths or marching through seas on dry land. Probably no one here today will bleed to death on the point of a spear. But many of you honestly and earnestly believe in your hearts that Jesus Christ is the Savior of the world. You know He's your Savior. Remember that Christian faith has a sacrifice at the heart of it. It is based on a love that was stronger than death. It will cost you something before you're through. "But don't call me a hero," you say. "I'm no hero of the faith. Don't class me with Abraham or Noah or even with Jim Elliot. My name doesn't belong on that list." Doesn't it? The list isn't finished yet. It ends with these astonishing words: "All these won a glowing testimony to their faith, but they did not then and there receive the fulfilment of the promise. God had something better planned for our day, and it was not his plan that they should reach perfection without us" (Heb. 11:39–40 *Phillips*).

Without you—and Abel and Abraham and Rahab and all the crowd of people who were stoned and sawn in two—are we to believe that they will not reach perfection without the graduates of your class? That is what we are to believe. You who walk out of here today with Christ in your hearts qualify for that list.

Is that a little bit terrifying to you? How shall we find the courage to follow in such a train? I'll tell you how—and I found the answer in the twelfth chapter. "Surrounded then as we are by these serried ranks of witnesses, let us strip off everything that hinders us, as well as the sin which dogs our feet, and let us run the race that we have to run with patience, our eyes fixed on Jesus, the source and the goal of our faith" (vv. 1–2 *Phillips*). In times of nearly paralyzing fear and loneliness in the jungle, I have suddenly remembered these "serried ranks," and have thought that I heard them cheering for me. They're like spectators in an arena, watching for victory. You and I are in the race. Let us "run with resolution," the New English Bible says, "the race for which we are entered." Your race, don't forget, is not the same as Abraham's. It isn't the same as Jim Elliot's. There is something individual and incommunicable about yours, something which in this form does not occur in anyone else's life, a quality of faith known to God alone, but its source and its goal are exactly the same for all of us in that arena—Jesus Christ, Pioneer and Perfecter, Author and Finisher. That's where it comes from, that's where it's going. Thank God for all that has made you what you are. Thank Him for your parents and for this school and the education you've gotten here and the degree that will follow your name now. Remember that to whomsoever much is given, of him shall much be required. For visible things in a visible world you need visible qualifications. Your cap and gown, you recall, are symbols of obedience to academic discipline. For invisible things in an invisible world you need invisible qualifications. The Cross of Jesus Christ, which speaks of sacrifice, is the symbol of the obedience of faith. It is that Cross which changed the world, and it is that Cross which changes you and me. You can love your own life and end up by destroying it or you can choose the way of sacrifice, *my life for yours,* and change the world. By putting your trust in Abraham's God, by simple, daily, humble obedience such as has characterized Christians for thousands of years, you can have your name on that list.

Take with you today God's faithful promise found in Isaiah 41:10:

> So do not fear, for I am with you;
> do not be dismayed, for I am your God.
> I will strengthen you and help you;
> I uphold you with my righteous right hand.
>
> (NIV)

*I*t is my heart's desire to give you something to hold
onto for the rest of your lives. The question we need to
face is, What is a Christian supposed to do when terrible
things happen? We have two choices—trust God or defy Him.
We believe that God is God, He's still got the whole world in
His hands and knows exactly what He's doing, or we must
believe that He is not God and we are at the awful mercy of
mere chance.

Faith is a decision. It is not a deduction from the facts
around us. Faith is an act of the will, a choice based on the
unbreakable Word of a God Who cannot lie, and Who showed us
what love and obedience and sacrifice mean in the person of
Jesus Christ.

So now you're graduating. The prince of this world
approaches. God keep you from fear, from faltering, and from
faithlessness. Remember that the world is watching. What do
they see?

Elisabeth Elliot